The Millennium Jubilee

The Millennium Jubilee

Theological reflections towards the Year 2000

Brian Davies
Mary Grey
Ed O'Connell
Jim O'Keefe
Aloys Opiyo
Jon Sobrino
David Williamson

First published in 1996 by
CAFOD
Romero Close
Stockwell Road
London SW9 9TY

Reprinted 1997

Chapters 2, 3, 4 and 5, originally published in *Proclaim
Jubilee* (CAFOD 1987), have been amended and updated
for this edition.

ISBN 0 871549 55 8

Designed by Ex Cathedra 0171 323 5581

Printed by The Longdunn Press Ltd
Barton Manor
St Philips
Bristol
BS2 0RL

Contents

Other Millennium publications from CAFOD:

*The Fullness of Time: Sunday gospel meditations in preparation
for the new millennium*   **Joseph Donders**

*The Coming of the Third Millennium: a popular version of the
apostolic letter of John Paul II, Tertio Millennio Adveniente*

Introduction

Mary Grey

The celebration of the millennium – whatever may happen in the way of media hype and public spectacle – offers too important an opportunity for CAFOD to let it pass without the sort of reflection that Pope John Paul urges us to share in his Apostolic Letter *Tertio Millennio Adveniente* (TMA). For once we have had plenty of warning and a strategy outlined for the coming years of preparation.

In chapter 1 of this book Ed O'Connell outlines the action programme presented in TMA where we are all invited to respond to the Jubilee ideal presented in the Bible. We are helped to see what potential there is for making the connections between *what kind* of future the millennium ushers in and CAFOD's agenda. Chapter 2 by Aloys Opiyo shows clearly the comprehensive and radical nature of the Jubilee message, not just in the Hebrew Scriptures but also in the Gospels. Once we are alerted to the signs, we find that "the missionary programme of Jesus of Nazareth is shot through with Jubilee language". We are warned of the ever-present tendency to spiritualise Jesus's proclamation, as if it were not directly referring to the poor and the oppressed. Taking the message as a model for action, Aloys Opiyo spells out some of the implications for mission today.

In chapter 3 David Williamson examines the only text from the Hebrew Scriptures where there is evidence of the Jubilee laws being kept and considers – imaginatively – how Nehemiah would have recalled the ideals of Exodus. The point is that the law of God has to be applied to the needs of each succeeding generation: this is what Jesus did, and in the face of escalating poverty and interconnected oppression, this is what needs to be done today by each of us in our own context. David Williamson concludes that the world economy is in our hands to control: it is for us to bring about whatever changes we can to embody the Jubilee vision: "For God's Law has to be made practical and lived and trumpeted in every generation."

Jim O'Keefe's contribution is the fruit of a summer vacation he spent living among the Gabbra people of northern Kenya. These tribal people, with their "pagan" culture, are actually putting into practice every seven years some of the Old Testament ideals of Jubilee: they bear witness to the idea that everything is provided by God for all to share. They show the beginnings of a sensitivity to women's inferior social situation in that during Jubilee time women are allowed to speak in public. They also show us that once we recognise that the Spirit of God is present in everyone, whether Christian or pagan, be it Kenya or Britain, then the way we evangelise has to become much more sensitive to culture and context.

But how can we proclaim Jubilee without a clear vision of what is to be remedied? The Jesuit Liberation theologian from El Salvador, Jon Sobrino, insists that we confront the stark truth of today's world – that the majority live in unnecessary poverty, which must be denounced as structural sin. In characteristic fashion, he shows that the initial response of compassion must lead to conversion and only in this way to salvation. In this process it is the poor who are the mediators of God's forgiveness and who point the way to a vision of the Kingdom vastly different from that offered by the western way of life. Paradoxically, it is the poor who are the means of salvation for the rich. In his concluding section, Jon Sobrino sees El Salvador as a symbol of the Third World, which is crying out for a lasting Jubilee.

In the final contribution, Brian Davies focuses on the central theme of reconciliation and shows that this cannot be achieved "cheaply". Having recognised the extent to which the Christian community is implicated in structural sin – and TMA is remarkably honest about the Church's failings – we need through an appropriate ritual of reconciliation to celebrate liturgically our repentance and commitment to a reformed way of life.

Since its proclamation of Jubilee in 1987 CAFOD has been committed to the need to extend the celebration to all the hidden peoples of the earth, to the many unheard voices, and to the needs of the earth, the soil community itself. Since the UN Assembly in Beijing (1995), there has been a growing awareness of the suffering and poverty of women on a global scale. TMA (para 51) in its call for laying greater emphasis on the Church's preferential option for the poor and the outcast, includes specifically the rights of women. As the international debt crisis worsens, it is the lives of poor women who are most affected, as girl-children are sold into prostitution or child labour, and as women struggle across desertified land in search of drinking water for their families.

In 1995 Church women in Korea saw the limitations of the Korean Churches' Jubilee programme when it did not include a women's perspective. The idea had been to relate Jubilee to the reunification of Korea. But the women read Leviticus 25 more earnestly and insisted that the whole programme of Jubilee should be taken seriously.[1] This is an example of what Sobrino was referring to when he said "We receive from the poor". The Korean women wanted political, economic and eco-justice to be given a more inclusive meaning: the interconnections between poor women and the suffering of the earth have to be made clear. They must also figure prominently on any agenda for the millennium.

The biblical figure of Miriam, the prophet, who led the celebration after the Children of Israel had fled from the oppression of Pharaoh, is inspirational in this struggle. She is recreated by a Korean woman theologian as the dangerous memory of the dance of freedom. In what follows, Miriam stays in solidarity and expresses her hope for a changed future:

> *The wilderness is so rough and thus is so beautiful,*
> *the wilderness is so low and thus is not hidden,*
> *I would be buried here*
> *to look at coming generation*
> *whenever pear flowers blossom and fall*
> *people would remember me,*
> *I who did not die for power, but for liberty,*
> *I who was dancing in the wilderness wearing a white veil and falling like pear flowers.* [2]

Taking to heart the interconnections which all the writers make, within an ever-deepening vision of what is meant by a just millennium, CAFOD hopes that this book will be one small way of making concrete the agenda of TMA.

1. Kim Jeongsoo, "Peace, Reunification, Jubilee and Church women" in *In God's Image*, 14:3, 1995, p. 16.

2. Yani Yoo, "Sister Pear Flower" *ibid*, p. 31.

Towards a Just Millennium

Ed O'Connell SSC

The razzmatazz that will surround the New Millennium's Eve Party is best portrayed by the image of those jetting off on Concorde to catch the midnight hour in three different places around the world. Contrast the hype of that celebration with the hope brick-kiln workers might have, for they are amongst the poorest of the poor. Their hope for the new millennium would surely be an end to the vicious circle in which they live, of having no land or home, of being in debt and in slavery by being bonded labourers.

Where does that leave the majority of us? In our own way, we will bring in the new millennium, enjoying ourselves on the night, yet because of our Christian faith, we will be acutely aware that the origins of the millennium celebrations are in the events of the life of Jesus of Nazareth, the Christ. Already, however, I have heard people say they are fed up with Millennium talk and, by the time it comes, we may be well and truly sick of it. Yet, as Christians, should we not be challenged to share what we believe the millennium celebration could mean for the world? That way, at least there might be some hope around once the party is over.

One person has been very aware of this challenge. From the very beginning of his pontificate, John Paul II realised the importance of the millennium celebration as a teaching moment for the Church. In 1987 he wrote in his Encyclical Letter *Sollicitudo Rei Socialis:*

> *The present period of time, on the eve of the third Christian millennium, is characterized by a widespread expectancy, rather like a new "Advent", which to some extent touches everyone.*

Even then, when promoting the "duty of solidarity" as a moral obligation, he threw down the gauntlet:

> *True development cannot consist in the simple accumulation of wealth and in the greater availability of goods and services, if this is gained at the expense of the development of the peoples, and without due consideration for the social, cultural and spiritual dimensions of the human being.*

So it should not have been a surprise to us when in November 1994 the Pope produced the Apostolic Letter *Tertio Adveniente Millennio* ("The Coming of the Third Millennium"), in which he set out his "Jubilee" perspective for the millennium celebration and laid out a plan of action for the Catholic Church, inviting all to respond, working where possible with people of other Christian denominations and other faiths and with all people of goodwill.

Tertio Millennio Adveniente (TMA) is an apostolic letter which means business. It required a Vatican Commission to be set up to oversee the work ahead and each Bishops' Conference and every diocese have been challenged to take the content of the apostolic letter seriously. It is a very powerful universal call to action, based on the biblical understanding of Jubilee, which "characterizes all the activity of Jesus" (para 11). The Jubilee concept of Old Testament times was there as a help to the people – first, after seven years to let the land lie fallow so as not to overwork it, hence the name "sabbatical", and to allow the poor and the stranger to take their pickings off the land. Then, after seven times seven years, the Jubilee Year, when those amongst the people of Israel who had been dispossessed of their land had the opportunity to regain it, those who were in debt had it cancelled, and those who had fallen into slavery were freed. This was a reminder to the people that all things belonged to God and were a gift for them to use; and the restoration of things after fifty years was a call to them to live in righteousness, that is, in right relations, with each other.

This Jubilee theme was central to Jesus' understanding of how things should be. Let us look briefly at an instance in his life to see how Jesus implemented the Jubilee in his teaching. The Last Judgement scene of Matthew (25:31-46) sees Jesus put flesh and blood on to the more idealistic Jubilee concepts of land, debt and slavery. He made them come alive when he spoke of people who were hungry, thirsty, strangers, naked, sick or in prison.

His description of them fits almost perfectly the situation of a homeless person, a refugee or an asylum seeker today. "In truth, I tell you, in so far as you did this to one of the least, you did it to me" is as relevant a spiritual message for the needs of today's world as it was then.

The Pope's agenda, which comes out of this Jubilee perspective, is clearly expressed in TMA:

> *If we recall that Jesus came to "preach the good news to the poor" (Mt 11:5; Lk 7:22), how can we fail to lay greater emphasis on the Church's preferential option for the poor and the outcast? Indeed, it has to be said that a commitment to justice and peace in a world, like ours, marked by so many conflicts and intolerable social and economic injustices, is a necessary condition for the preparation and celebration of the Jubilee. Thus, in the spirit of the Book of Leviticus (25:8-12), Christians will have to raise their voice in appropriate time to give thought, among other things, to reducing substantially, if not cancelling outright, the international debt which seriously threatens the future of many nations. The Jubilee can also offer an opportunity for reflecting on other challenges of our time, such as the difficulties of dialogue between different cultures and the problems of the family and marriage. (para 51)*

A framework for action

In chapter 4 of the apostolic letter the Pope sets out a framework for action.

Phase One: Pre-preparation

The years 1995 and 1996 were designated as a time for examination of conscience, particularly with regard to the events of the last one hundred years, to see how Christians had lived up to their name and mission. These years are to help people to take seriously a time of preparation for the millennium and to give thanks for the main Church event of this century, the Second Vatican Council. There is a positive and educational value in the way this section holds up before the universal Church the need to repent the role played by Christians in the increase and spread of poverty and to confess, as sinful, the silent acceptance of the legitimacy of amassed wealth and over-consumption in the face of devastating global poverty and suffering.

Phase Two: The Advent Years of Preparation

These years, based on the theme of the Trinity, are action years. It is best to take the three years as a unit and apply the criterion for each year – 1997 of working ecumenically, 1998 of finding signs of hope and 1999 of reaching out for reconciliation – as overall criteria for action during the whole three-year Advent period of preparation for the Year 2000.

1997 concentrates upon the person of Jesus Christ, his baptism and mission to bring about the Jubilee of Justice (Lk 4:19). It offers the perfect base for ecumenical action. 1998 centres around the activity of the Holy Spirit and highlights confirmation as a call to give witness to our faith and we are challenged to name the signs of hope we see around us and build on them. 1999 focuses on God the Father and stresses the unconditional love of God for every person, hence reconciliation. This love is the ultimate theological foundation for universal human rights and a call for the elimination of poverty, requiring redistribution of property and relief from the burden of debt – in other words, the living out of the Jubilee.

Jubilee Year: 2000

The year 2000 is to be intensely Eucharistic. During this year, the Church around the world should work to overcome the dramatic gaps between people and bring divided people around the same table: wealthy and poor, North and South, employed and unemployed, peoples divided by cultures, fears and discriminations ... the list could be endless. And perhaps as a great dramatic gesture of thanks and praise to God, the Church could commit itself to work with other Christian denominations, other faiths, governments and people of goodwill everywhere towards ending hunger wherever it remains upon the earth during the Jubilee Year.

We are not starting from scratch in our efforts to respond to the framework of action presented to us by TMA. For a number of years CAFOD and other non-government organisations (NGOs) have been stressing the need to break the cycle of the current "economy of exclusion". If the main issues of poverty in the social structures of their countries are to be truly faced then development must be characterised by economic justice, ecological sustainability and participatory social and political processes. CAFOD, with its sister Catholic agencies, submitted the following principles and proposals to the Summit for Social Development held in Copenhagen in March 1995, which they believe lie at the foundation of any successful response to the contemporary social crisis:

1. *Respect for human rights as the foundation of authentic social development.*
2. *Improved indicators and measures of development.*
3. *The fostering of strong and active participation in civil society.*
4. *The provision of basic needs and the means of production essential to participation in civil society.*
5. *The removal of the debt burden and destructive economic restructuring programmes.*
6. *Over-consumption and other forms of bad development challenged.*

I would add a seventh:

7. *Effective mechanisms put in place to curb the arms trade as a contribution to minimising violent social disintegration.*

These points are not only a basis for our awareness-raising and campaigning work, they are also the focal points for our compassion and solidarity with the poor of the world. They relate well to the criteria for CAFOD's 1000 projects in Africa, Asia, Latin America and Eastern Europe. In the words of Cardinal Basil Hume, "CAFOD is an expression of solidarity, of love, of our yearning for justice for the poor in the developing world." CAFOD is in a unique position to promote the framework of action which TMA offers from now until the millennium.

Let us look briefly at what CAFOD is proposing for their special Millennium Programme:

Working with dioceses, parishes, organisations and schools in England and Wales, CAFOD is seeking to help implement the Pope's call by formalising the commitment of the local Churches to poor communities around the world, through "A New Covenant with the Poor". This new covenant will express and strengthen the Church's mission of being the bearer of good news to the poor. It is a real, and at the same time symbolic, redistribution of the wealth of the world through CAFOD projects. The hope is that each diocese will consider such a covenant as one part of its Advent Year preparations for the millennium in 1997, and that subsequently parishes, Catholic organisations, schools, families and individuals might make their own covenants.

CAFOD will be part of a developing campaign network to increase understanding and generate action for change around the Jubilee themes of cancelling debt and improving working conditions – freeing people from a slave-like way of life. Through its Campaigns and Fast Days between 1997 and 2001 CAFOD will echo Pope John Paul's call for repentance for the way we have impoverished others in the past and his exhortation to seek out justice for the poor. In January 1997 a CAFOD Campaign will be launched on "Just Work– Fair Play", reflecting on the way labour has been exploited in the Third World through slave-like practices as well as the misery of continual unemployment. Along with others CAFOD will focus increasingly on the debt crisis, seeking a means for the Churches to apply pressure for a Third World debt reduction.

CAFOD wants people to meet as equals. Hence the "Pilgrim People" project of "exposure visits" by people of all ages from England and Wales to experience the partnership between CAFOD and poor communities at work in other parts of the world and to share this experience with others on their return. In the Year 2000 some of CAFOD's partners worldwide will make visits to parishes in England and Wales, to deepen the partnership further and to celebrate the Millennium together.

CAFOD is planning an "Option for Young People", and hopes to work in co-operation with Catholic Youth Services and diocesan youth organisations to create programmes that will foster Justice and Peace as a real and relevant option requiring decision and action by young adults today and into the next millennium. This is a practical response to the call of Pope John Paul II, who in the conclusion of TMA asked the young people of today to take up the challenge of being the bearers of the Good News into the first century of the next millennium. This endeavour needs all our support and I am delighted CAFOD has taken a lead with this initiative.

As a tangible way of sharing its millennium celebration with the Third World, CAFOD hopes to secure additional financial resources from Trusts and Lottery-related sources to enable partners to achieve some of their specific Jubilee objectives that might not otherwise be possible.

CAFOD will also produce materials to support prayer and reflection which relate to the Trinitarian and Jubilee themes of the preparatory years. This should help those who are seeking a spirituality which holds together issues of poverty and injustice with their life of prayer.

So now it is back to each and everyone of us to get involved at parish and local level and from there contribute to our diocesan programmes, so that they reflect the true nature of Jubilee. Then nationally, in coordination with the Bishops' Conference, and through CAFOD, campaign on issues which affect the life of "the poor and outcast". If we manage this, with the grace of God, we shall be doing our best to bring the Jubilee way into the next millennium, and this goes well beyond what any party could hope to reach!

Jubilee: A Model for Mission

Aloys Opiyo

The Bible's central theme is that God takes human life and human history seriously, so seriously that he sent his only begotten son to take part in it, to suffer from it, to die for it, to bring redemption to it. If we examine more closely Jesus' teaching about the Kingdom – and in particular his manifesto in Luke 4: "to proclaim the Lord's year of favour" – we will discern direct references to the Old Testament teaching on the Jubilee, when once in every 50 years land was to be redistributed and every family, every tribe, given the chance to make a new beginning. Just as this was based not on merit but on a purely gratuitous reordering of things, so the Kingdom announced by Jesus is offered as a free gift by God, who gives each of his children the opportunity to make a new beginning in life.

We shall also discover that the Jubilee model expands the horizon for Christian mission in the world today, pointing as it does to the universality of the Kingdom of God, which was for Jesus, as it should be for us, the all-embracing objective of mission (Lk 4:43).

This is particularly relevant for a world that is struggling to ward off the threat of destruction and urgently searching for human liberation at every level. The quest for survival and the desire to improve the quality of life around the world demand a vision of mission that will match the extent of our present crisis and the magnitude of the gospel promise.

In recent decades thinking about mission has been inspired by a variety of biblical concepts: "the apostolate", "the sending God", "*missio Dei*", "God's *shalom*", the Exodus paradigm of liberation. The Jubilee model has not been a source of inspiration to the same extent, but there is no doubt about its potential for giving a common focus to those aspects of Christian faith, theology and mission that tend to be kept apart: creation and redemption, the Kingdom of God and the human global village, mission and secular tasks of construction and reconstruction.

The programmatic message of Jesus

Jesus' inaugural message, especially the verses in Luke 4:18-19, has become a favoured text for preachers in Latin America and other parts of the Third World, who emphasise his reference to liberation and the holistic character of his message, and of our mission today. But frequent quotation is infrequently supported by adequate analysis of the text. A fruitful attempt has been made by Thomas Hanks, professor of biblical studies at the Seminario Biblico Latinoamericano in San Jose, Costa Rica. His book, *Oppression, Poverty and Liberation*, is a notable example of how liberated and liberating a biblical, scientific and contextual analysis can be.

Contemporary Lucan scholars recognise that Luke 4:14-44 serves as a prologue to the author's literary and theological enterprise, which begins with Jesus' inaugural proclamation of the Kingdom in Nazareth, continues with the Kingdom talks after the resurrection, and reaches its climax with Paul's proclamation of the Kingdom of God, "from morning until evening", "openly and unhindered", for two full years in the capital city of the caesars (Lk 4:43; Acts 28:23,31).

Luke, of course, is not alone in taking this as his starting point. In Mark's account of the Gospel, the curtain rises on Jesus' initial proclamation of the coming Kingdom: "Jesus came into Galilee, proclaiming the Gospel of the Kingdom of God and saying: 'The time is fulfilled and the Kingdom of God is at hand: repent and believe in the Gospel'" (Mk 1:14-15). And the same is true of the gospel of Matthew, which confirms both the content of the message and the Galilean context: "He went about all Galilee, teaching in their synagogues and preaching the Gospel of the Kingdom" (Mt 4:23).

What is unique in the Lucan version is this specific connection of the kingdom Gospel with the prophetic proclamation of the Jubilee Year, "the Lord's year of favour". And this becomes Jesus' own definition of his mission: "I must proclaim the good news of the Kingdom of God to other cities too; for I was sent for this purpose" (Lk 4:43).

Jesus came to announce the Kingdom of God and he did it in jubilee language in order to define his mission. We ourselves cannot escape the implications of this when we define our own mission in the world today.

> *He came to Nazara, where he had been brought up, and went into the synagogue on the sabbath day as he usually did. He stood up to read, and they handed him the scroll of the prophet Isaiah. Unrolling the scroll he found the place where it is written:*
>
> *"The Spirit of the Lord has been given to me, for he has anointed me.*
> *He has sent me to bring the good news to the poor,*
> *to proclaim liberty to captives,*
> *and to the blind new sight,*
> *to set the downtrodden free,*
> *to proclaim the Lord's year of favour."*
>
> *He then rolled up the scroll, gave it back to the assistant and sat down. And all eyes in the synagogue were fixed on him. Then he began to speak to them,*
>
> *"This text is being fulfilled today even as you listen."*
> *(Lk 4:16-21)*

According to the third gospel, this was Jesus' first revelation of his identity and his mission. Quoting from Isaiah 61:1-2 and 58:6, he identified himself with the herald prophet, anointed by the Spirit of the Lord to announce the good tidings of "the Lord's year of favour".

This was the language of visions and eschatological promises used by Isaiah after the bitter experiences of the exile. And Jesus was using it in the presence of his townspeople to make the incredible affirmation that such promises and hopes of the end of time were being fulfilled right there, before their eyes and in his own person: "This text is being fulfilled today even as you listen!"

Jesus and the Scriptures

We can feel the spell cast by Jesus from the few hints Luke gives us: "And all eyes in the synagogue were fixed on him", "and he won the approval of all, and they were astonished by the gracious words that came from his lips." No wonder. Jesus was applying to himself words that the prophets and teachers of Qumram expected would be fulfilled with the apocalyptic coming of Melchisedech, surrounded by his heavenly host, at the end of time, with the destruction of the armies of darkness and the victory of the children of light represented by the faithful community of Qumram.

They were perplexed: their reaction was ambivalent. In verse 22 they are still a listening congregation, but seven verses later they have become an angry mob. What brought about the transformation was not Jesus' wisdom or his work but his specific application of Isaiah's words to himself, and in particular his understanding of God's dealings with the "pagan" peoples beyond Israel's borders – in short, his prophetic challenge to the chosen people. In a word, what angered the people of Nazareth was the way Jesus interpreted the Scriptures. So much so, in fact, that his mission nearly ended as it was beginning, with his untimely death over the brow of a hill. Jesus left his town never to come back.

We must therefore suspect that there is more in this passage than meets the eye. Some have suggested that Jesus was given these verses to read from the lectionary of the day, others that he "found" them by chance. But there is nothing fortuitous or casual here. Jesus' selection of these particular verses and his comments and applications are quite deliberate. His message at the synagogue is totally consistent with his proclamation of the Kingdom of God, with his understanding of himself and his mission, and with his peculiar use of the jubilee motif.

Jesus' contemporaries were not alone in being puzzled by his free use of the Scriptures. It has also puzzled biblical scholars over the years. For instance, Jesus stopped his quotation of Isaiah 61:1-2 half way through verse 2, thus ending with the words "to proclaim the Lord's year of favour", and leaving out the phrase "a day of vengeance of our God". The omission is intriguing and significant: it emphasises the dimension of grace in his proclamation of "the Lord's year of favour". But no less intriguing and significant is his addition of the key words from Isaiah 58:6: "to let the oppressed go free". Now it has been convincingly demonstrated, that Isaiah 58 is a jubilee chapter, beginning with the Day of Atonement and describing true fasting in terms of liberating the oppressed. God's liberation from sin and debt has to be received and expressed through liberation of neighbour:

> *Is not this the sort of fast that pleases me:*
> *to break unjust fetters,*
> *and undo the thongs of the yoke,*
> *to let the oppressed go free,*
> *and to break every yoke?*
> *(Is 58:6)*

Liberating human actions are the only adequate response to the jubilary and liberating grace of the Lord.

The missionary programme of Jesus in Nazareth is shot through with jubilee language and eschatological projections. For example, the proclamation of "release to the captives" is a prophetic projection from Leviticus 25:10, where the Jubilee Year is established: "You will declare this fiftieth year sacred and proclaim the liberation of all the inhabitants of the land."

The Hebrew word for liberation is used only seven times in the Old Testament and always in relation to the Jubilee Year. It was the term used by the prophets to indicate the year of the Jubilee, the year of release, the year of liberation (Jer 34:8, 15, 17; Ez 46:17; Is 61:1). It is this very word, translated as "release" and "liberty", that links Isaiah 61:1-2 and Isaiah 58:6. And it is obviously the key word in the Jubilee proclamation of Jesus in Nazareth.

As far as the Greek text is concerned the word for "release" and "liberation" is used 50 times in the Septuagint version of the Old Testament – 22 of them in jubilee passages in Leviticus 25 and 27. Liberation is the key word for Jesus' message and for his mission.

The same can be said of the expression "favourable (or acceptable) year of the Lord", which becomes the equivalent of the Jubilee Year and the model for the inauguration of the Kingdom of God in Jesus of Nazareth. What, then, is the meaning of Jubilee, and what are the implications of the jubilee motifs in the Old and New Testaments?

The Jubilee Year

Jubilee comes from *yobel*, the Hebrew word which had come to be applied to the ram's horn that was used to announce the Jubilee Year (Ex 19:13). Its original meaning, however, was liberation, as prescribed in Leviticus 25, to be celebrated every seven periods of seven years (on the forty-ninth or the fiftieth year).

The central provision of the jubilee code was that people should return periodically to the lands of their tribes and families (Lev 25:13, 28, 31). The purpose of this was to preserve the original agrarian democracy in Israel, and it was consistent with the projected just and fraternal society of the Covenant, the new order founded on the justice of the liberating and providing God. The periodic redistribution of land could correct the injustice whereby impoverished small farmers had to sell their lands, and even their families, to pay taxes and cover debts run up after natural disasters such as drought, sickness or death, and social disasters like royal expropriations and foreign invasions. To be deprived of land was to be deprived of freedom – and life itself.

Further laws with jubilee implications were laid down by the Holiness Code: (1) land was to lie fallow every seven years (Lev 25:1-7, 18-22); (2) land was to be valued according to the number of crops harvested on it since the previous Jubilee Year (25:14-17); (3) the original owner of a piece of land, or a member of his family, could redeem it from the person to whom it had been sold at any time between two jubilee years (25:23-28); (4) usury and the exploitation of an impoverished Hebrew brother was forbidden (25:35-38); (5) slaves were to be emancipated every seven years, in any year, not necessarily a sabbatical or jubilee year (25:39-43), and a Hebrew slave could be redeemed at any time, once economic compensation had been made (25:47-53); (6) there was to be an obligatory and unconditional liberation of slaves during the Jubilee Year (25:54-55).

The use of the land was granted by God himself and no one should sell it in perpetuity:

> *Land must not be sold in perpetuity,*
> *for the land belongs to me,*
> *and to me you are only strangers and guests.*
> *You will allow a right of redemption*
> *on all your landed property.*
> *(Lev 25:23-24)*

Ownership, in this biblical jubilee perspective, is not absolute, without limits or forever. Or as Pope John Paul II put it more recently, "property has a social mortgage". In other words, God is the only absolute owner, and his land is for all his children, to support life and guarantee human freedom and dignity, "You must put my laws and customs into practice; you must keep them, practise them; and so you shall be secure in your possession of the land" (Lev 25:18). Provisions for the redistribution of land and the welfare of impoverished people are founded on God's past mercy and his present sovereignty:

> *I am the Lord your God,*
> *who brought you out of the land of Egypt*
> *to give you the land of Canaan*
> *and to be your God.*
> *(Lev 25:38)*

> *For they are my servants,*
> *these whom I brought out of Egypt;*
> *and they must not be sold like slaves.*
> *(Lev 25:42)*

Nobody is absolute owner of the land, much less of human lives.

God's revolution or utopian vision?

This vision of a Jubilee Year – desired by God, established by law, proclaimed by the prophets – may appear utopian to us. And sceptics ask whether the Jubilee legislation was ever applied. It is of course difficult to prove that it was ever universally applied at any stage in the history of Israel. There is evidence, however, that it was applied partially and circumstantially. For instance, King Zedekiah's manumission of slaves, under the influence of the prophet Jeremiah, during the Babylonian siege of Jerusalem (Jer 34). The treatment of slaves was a recurrent theme in the prophet's preaching (verses 12-17) and the King's action was a sign of repentance and submission to God's will at a time of crisis. The Jubilee demand for the emancipation of slaves was a decisive yardstick. That the ruling class in Jerusalem first "obeyed and set them free" and then later "turned around and took them back" has two things to tell us: that human greed leaves no room for Jubilees, but that on the other hand the Jubilee ideal was written in the consciences of "all the princes and all the people who had entered into the Covenant" (verses 8-11). The same can be said of Nehemiah's dramatic application of the Jubilee in the community of those who had returned from the Exile (see the chapter by David Williamson following).

It is significant that the Jubilee legislation is present in all the strata of the Mosaic Law: in the Holiness Code of Leviticus, as we have seen, in the Covenant

Code of Exodus, and in the Deuteronomic version of the Law. In Exodus 21:2-6, for example, provision is made for the release of all Hebrew slaves every seven years – the theological principle being that people, like land, belong, not to other people, but to God. The provision in Exodus 23:10-11 for a sabbath year, during which the land was to be allowed to lie fallow, for social as well as for religious and ecological reasons, is affirmed in Deuteronomy 15, where it is described as a "year of remission" or "release":

> *Now the nature of the remission is this:*
> *every creditor who holds the person of his*
> *neighbour in bond must grant his remission; he*
> *may not exact payment from his fellow or his*
> *brother once the latter appeals to Yahweh for*
> *remission.*
> *(Deut 15:1-2)*

This introduces a new feature. God's children are to acknowledge the fact that he has forgiven them by cancelling debts among themselves. This is the appropriate way to respond to God's grace (verses 14-15). It was this theme of holistic atonement that Isaiah subsequently developed (chapter 58), and that Jesus incorporated into his own proclamation of the Jubilee – "the Lord's year of favour", the new beginning.

How should we interpret Jesus' proclamation?

One way of interpreting Jesus proclamation at Nazareth is to spiritualise it. The "poor" for whom Jesus brought "good news" are the spiritually poor. The "captives" are those who are captives of sin. The "blind" are those who do not know the Gospel. The "oppressed" are the spiritually oppressed, the slaves of sin.

There is a good deal of truth in this interpretation (cf Lk 24:47; Acts 10:38). According to the gospels, sin is rooted in the human heart and is the source of all evil. But we need to spell out the meaning and the scope of sin, its social and structural dimensions, for as Paul says: "We are not contending against flesh and blood, but against the principalities, against the powers, against the world rulers of this present darkness" (Eph 6:12).

In addition to spiritualising, we have a tendency to generalise and in so doing to lose sight of specific abuses. Yet, if Jesus was talking only of spiritual liberation and of sin in general, how do you explain the angry reaction of his fellow-citizens? Jesus was not rejected for mouthing spiritual platitudes, he was not nailed to the cross for talking about sin in general. The powers that be are happy enough for people to preach a "spiritual gospel", and those who do so have no problem with dictatorships and repressive regimes – on the contrary, they enjoy all kinds of cooperation.

There is another major gap in this spiritual interpretation of Jesus' Jubilee proclamation. We refer to sinners, but seldom to the sinned against. We recall that we are all sinners and forget about the victims of sin and of sinful structures – Jesus is challenging us to think again. His jubilee message is an offer of grace, of forgiveness for sinners, certainly, but look again at the list of those to whom it is addressed: "the poor", "the broken-hearted", "the captives", "the blind", "the oppressed" – in other words, the sinned against.

Careful study of the words "oppression" and "poverty" in the Bible leads to two conclusions. First, that "poverty" is the result of "oppression" rather than of chance, destiny or "under-development"! And second, that the words chosen by Jesus in Luke 4:18-19 are in fact an impressionistic description of the human situation and, more concretely, a comprehensive picture of the poor. The four words used: "poor", "captives", "blind" and "oppressed", simply refer to four faces of the one reality which is poverty.

Then there are some who interpret Jesus' message literally – as inaugurating a Jubilee Year that was due to take place in Palestine in the year 26 AD. According to this view, Jesus' sudden demand that the law be put into effect by "expropriations" and "liquidating the usurious system" was a call for the restoration of the "jubilean practices". Naturally this stirred up the enthusiasm of the poor and provoked the rage of the rich landowners and money lenders, which explains the mixed reception Jesus got in the synagogue of Nazareth.

Finally, there is a third possibility. Instead of interpreting Jubilee spiritually or literally, we can take it as a model for action, using it to develop a vision and model of mission in the Kingdom perspective. In other words as a dynamic working utopia, a biblical utopia – utopia being understood as an "expression of hope", "a passion for things yet to be", a critical approach to things "as they are". It is within this last perspective that we dare to make some brief and tentative suggestions for mission today.

Mission as Jubilee proclamation

Mission as liberation

The liberation in question here is total: historical and eternal, material and spiritual. It involves liberation from all forms of social and economic oppression, and liberation, through forgiveness, from the root cause of oppression, the inner bondage of sin.

This forgiveness is twofold: we receive it from God as forgiveness of sins and give it to our neighbours by cancelling their debts, following Jesus' teaching in the parable of the unforgiving servant and in the Lord's prayer: "Forgive our sins as we forgive those who are indebted to us" (Mt 18:23-25; 6:12, 14).

But just as Jesus' proclamation of liberation did not stop with the forgiveness of sins, but went on to include liberation from sickness and false relationships, so mission cannot be limited to the ministry of absolution – to "the power of the keys" for verbal confession. We are called to declare God's total release.

Today that means what the Synod on Evangelisation called liberation from "all forms of oppression" – poverty, discriminatory landholding laws and practices, injustices within the international economic system. The problem of hunger will not be solved with bullets or with ballots! As the Jubilee legislation reminds us, without land and stock, liberated slaves simply fall back into slavery. The aim of mission is liberation of the oppressed.

Mission as rectification

Part of our task will be to rectify the personal and social order, to announce the year of God's amendment which is what Jubilee and the atonement are all about. Because sin produces social inequalities, society needs periodically to be restructured.

Jesus came proclaiming a topsy-turvy kingdom where the last will be first and the first last. We need to reread the beatitudes and the parables with jubilee eyes. The announcement of the reign of God, of the new order, of God's amendment, comes with a call to repentance: "The time is fulfilled; the Kingdom is at hand – repent!" – not only personally but socially, nationally, collectively, to bring everybody and everything into line with the Kingdom.

The Jubilee – like experience – suggests that this is an ongoing task. It has to be taken up again and again. There will be no permanent order, no final revolution, until mission reaches its consummation in the Kingdom. In this sense, to be in mission is to be in revolution.

Naturally, this involves searching questions and painful options. As Christians we cannot avoid revolution. What we have to ask ourselves is: where is this particular revolution going? will it help to rectify injustices? will it represent, like the Jubilee, "a moment of justice" in history? Unless we get rid of "institutional violence", we will be faced, as Dom Helder Camara has warned us, with revolutionary and repressive violence.

No society can go on indefinitely without rectification. Not even the Church is exempt from this rule. Mission is carried out by a pilgrim Church in a changing world, and the message for individuals, institutions and societies is *repent!*

Mission as restoration

The Jubilee was a proclamation of renewal: the restoration of individuals, of social relationships, of nature itself. Economic justice and ecological balance are integral to the Jubilee proclamation.

Once again, it is a matter of faith and human endeavour. Christians, along with the rest of the human community, are partners under God in the delicate stewardship of creation. This mission has no frontiers: whenever we struggle for justice and for environmental responsibility we are engaged in mission. Jesus' ministry was a jubilee ministry for the restoration of life and for the announcement of the fullness of life. And he sent his disciples to announce life, to defend life, to restore life, to celebrate life.

Our task, then, is to announce the good news of life, the restoration of life, "until he comes", "until the end comes" – an end which is exclusively in God's hands, and which we may not precipitate by neglect, irresponsibility, rebellion or demonic madness. The task is to announce the good news of life, the restoration of life, and then in God's time "will come the end" (Mt 24:14).

Mission as inauguration

Finally, mission is inauguration, anticipation, annunciation of the new year of the Lord. The Jubilee was never intended to recover a golden age of the past. Rather, it looked forward to an eschatological future, to the messianic times, to "the Lord's year of favour" proclaimed and promised by the prophets. What Jesus did was to take hold of the substance of their visions and proclaim its inauguration here and now, in the coming of the Kingdom of God: "The time is fulfilled, the Kingdom of God has arrived." But if the inaugural message of Nazareth is a point of arrival, it is also a new point of departure.

Jesus invited his disciples to "enter" into the Kingdom, to join the movement of the Kingdom by preaching, teaching, healing, forgiving, serving, loving, building – now. They were to wait for its consummation not in idleness, destructive consumerism and social irresponsibility, but in caring behaviour and responsible stewardship (Lk 12:41-48; Mt 25). The Lord will come, but meanwhile he is at work and has called us to work with him.

The Church participates in the tasks of the in-breaking Kingdom and celebrates in anticipation of its final consummation. The Kingdom is both experience and hope – experience of forgiveness, of transforming love and of the presence and power of the Holy Spirit, hope of fulfilment in the midst of the frustrations, fragmentations and ambiguities of history, in the midst of suffering and death.

While we walk with this experience and this hope, we are called to provoke temporary and partial jubilees, "moments of justice", here and there, in the Church and in society. Even if the world is resistant and the Church frequently opaque, we must not let the dream go stale. Because when we dream, it is God who dreams in us. Our mission is to inaugurate new ways, new experiments, new signs of the coming Kingdom. And we are called to start with ourselves and with the Church, adventuring in new styles of life, new gestures, new beginnings.

Both the rich young man and Zaccheus were challenged to take concrete steps in relation to their possessions and their social responsibilities. The one was unable to enter into his own jubilee and went away sorrowful; the other responded with a bold and creative gesture that marked a new beginning. He tasted the "Lord's year of favour" and salvation came to his house (Mt 19:16-22; Lk 19:1-10). Zaccheus knew the joy and the tasks of inauguration.

Mission is inauguration: let's blow the trumpet!

Blowing our own Trumpet

David Williamson

Imagine a ruined land – arid, neglected, supporting little but worthless weeds. Here and there the old markers that separated farm from farm are still standing, but most have fallen flat or disappeared completely. Few of the ditches that kept the fields watered are still working; fewer still of the ancient cisterns that saved the rains.

Across this land a group of people hurries towards the town; they are singing a song.

> *When Israel came forth from Egypt,*
> *Jacob's sons from an alien people,*
> *Judah became the Lord's temple,*
> *Israel became his kingdom.*
> *(Ps 114:1-2)*

The tune is cheerful, but their faces and their stride say that they are angry. They are singing one of the freedom songs of their people, but they are not free.

Market forces

Once in the town the group stops at the mayor's house. In fact the title given him by the Persian

King of Kings is much grander than that, but compared with the other satraps and governors, who have more people to rule than they can count, he is just a mayor. He is rather a grim man, more than a little self-opinionated and not much less self-righteous. His name is Nehemiah.

Nehemiah already knows what the crowd wants; he has not spent a lifetime in the civil service without learning what people will put up with, and what pushes them beyond endurance. These people have been pushed too far, and will soon be ready to riot, perhaps to kill.

Nehemiah's problem was that he sympathised with this crowd: they had justice on their side. Yet what could he do to change things? You cannot make food grow simply by willing it to do so, or even keeping God's holy laws. Food grows when people with know-how make it grow; and the people with know-how are the people with money -- and land! The crowd was right: the rent they paid in grain was too high, leaving them barely enough to feed themselves; loan and mortgage repayments were so steep it was impossible to avoid bankruptcy, and after bankruptcy came "indentured service", a sweet phrase meaning bitter slavery. Indeed, many of their sons and daughters were already slaves. Jews owning Jewish slaves! By the oil of Aaron's beard – how could the people of the Exodus sink to buying and selling their own kin! And yet, the interest rate was no higher than among pagans, the rents were the same, and so was the price of food. If he insisted on prices the people could afford the food would just be sold elsewhere. If he changed the interest rate the supply of credit would dry up: there were plenty in Moab and Edom over the river who would borrow at these rates without complaint. And then where would his poor be?

He heard their complaint, and felt the violence filling them. And he promised that he would give all the help possible; it would not be everything they wanted, but it would be the most that could be done. "Go home," he told them, "tomorrow is the tenth day of the seventh month, the Day of Atonement. Blow your trumpets, and when everyone, rich and poor together, has arrived at the site of the Temple I will tell you the decision."

Ancient memories

Back in his house Nehemiah opened his Torah scroll. Had he been using a modern Bible, he would have turned to the Book of Exodus, chapters 21-23. These pages contain the first laws written down by the people of Israel, when, having escaped from slavery, they came into their own land. This legal code, the constitution of their nation, was very different, in its mood and in its precepts, from the legal code of the surrounding nations. These other nations – we can still read many of their law-codes today – based their system of justice on rank and wealth. For example, if a rich aristocrat wronged a poor labourer, the aristocrat would be ordered to pay the labourer ten pence. But if it was the other way about, the labourer would have to pay the aristocrat ten pounds! Such societies were harsh on the unfortunate, who usually ended up as slaves. And while slavery in Assyria or Babylon was less brutal than it was in Rome, it nevertheless meant the end of all hopes of independence, family and home.

The new-born nation of Israel would not have anyone condemned to such hopelessness. Having once been slaves themselves, the Israelites made laws to ensure that no one else would. They knew it was impossible to eliminate poverty altogether, and therefore impossible, even in Israel, to abolish every form of slavery: but the hopelessness could go! Under the law, no Israelite could be made a slave. Those most at risk – immigrants, the homeless, orphans and widows – could be taken on to work under contract for six years, but after that, no matter what their state of debit or credit, free they went. And if this freedom came in a year of disaster, with food shortages, drought and therefore no other job to go to, the man was to be taken into the home for ever, not as a slave, but with a ceremony to make him a full member of the family. And what of women? Israel must have seen appalling things happen to women in hardship, for the law is remarkable: in a world where women were bought and sold more easily than oxen, the Torah says that no woman may be made a slave. Once a woman left her father's home she became a wife or a daughter-in-law in a new home, or else she was given complete freedom.

But the ancient law at the beginning of the search for freedom was even more remarkable for the fact that it treated rich and poor equally. A rich man who injured a poor man's eye had the same injury done to his own eye. What a revolution! The rich can make financial compensation and have money to spare, but they have the same number of eyes, or arms, or legs as the poor. The rich we have always with us, but how well Israel tempered their arrogance.

And now Nehemiah in his reading became sad, for he had reached what for us is Exodus 23:10-11:

> *For six years you shall sow your land and gather in its yield; but in the seventh year you shall let it rest and lie fallow, that the poor of your people may eat.*

How accurately the ancestors had understood their place in God's world. Not as owners, but as stewards, with God as the sole owner of all the land. And, just as God, the rescuer of the slave, gave the use of his land to the oppressed and the destitute, to Israel, so Israel, each seventh year, put aside the rights of stewardship, and left the harvest for the poorest in the community. With the seed of grain as well as the grain for immediate eating, this seventh year harvest could have been a considerable endowment, setting up the destitute for independence. What a law for freedom! Nehemiah turned his scroll.

When the good times came

He stopped this time at Deuteronomy, at our fifteenth chapter, but glancing beyond it to laws about the merciful treatment of enemies, and about keeping control over the antics of the king.

These parts of Deuteronomy are thought to have been written towards the end of the monarchy of Judah, when the memory of being a wealthy empire had not quite faded, and when prosperity and power seemed to be on their way back (what Nehemiah would have thought of our modern ways of dating his Torah we cannot know). In that fifteenth chapter Nehemiah found his "seven-year freedom rule" again, but in a very different form. Contemporary researchers would want to suggest to the old mayor that the law was different because times had changed. It had been written down more than a century before he was born, and more than 400 years after the first laws he had read.

In times of prosperity and flourishing commerce people depend less on owning land and more on controlling money. Consequently those with wealth to lend do it in the form of money, rather than of fields of grain. But, land or money, it is all the same from the debtor's point of view and leads to the same destitution.

And so the law that God had inspired about owning the land was extended to owning money: the Israelites were its stewards, not its owners, and every seventh year they gave back their stewardship into God's hands. Of course, God absolved the debts, as he always did.

A duty to lend

The rules for this seventh year cancellation of all debts are fascinating in their grasp of human nature. In was obvious that, as the seventh year drew near, some people, realising that there was little chance of their being repaid in the short time left, and that the loan in effect would be an outright gift, would be reluctant to lend their money to the utterly impoverished. With such reluctance in mind, the law still says:

> *You shall open your hand to him, and lend him sufficient for his need, whatever it may be. Take heed lest there be a base thought in your heart, and you say "The seventh year the year of release is near," and your eye be hostile to your brother, and you give him nothing and he cry to the Lord against you, and it be sin in you.*
> *(Deut 15:29)*

So, Nehemiah might have pondered, when the economic climate changes God's law must be thought out again so that it actually works in the new circumstances. The Holy Law commanded freedom for everyone; not an ideal freedom in some utopian future, but the best freedom possible in the real situation of real people. It might be impossible to abolish slavery and poverty totally, but the Israelites were not to get away with organising seminars and demonstrations about the ideal future freedom; they were to do their practical and commercial best to give the maximum freedom and independence possible in their own day.

Besides extending God's law to take account of money, Deuteronomy introduced a three-year tax payable by everyone with security to relieve the destitute. And for those who had slipped right through the net into slavery, not only was the seventh year freedom rule still in force, but a new rule had been enacted: on receiving his freedom the slave was to be given an endowment to help him set up on his own.

Life had changed for the women too. They had become economically independent of men, able to own property and trade in their own right. But that meant they could also go broke in their own right! What should happen then, since for a woman the life of slavery was as bad as our more lurid thoughts can imagine? The answer was that they were to have equal standing with men, to be treated the same, and to go free to run their own lives.

The trumpet day

Did Nehemiah read on? We cannot know. It may be that he had in his scroll what we call the Book of Leviticus, in which case he would certainly have wound on to our chapter 25. Or it may be that that part of Leviticus had not yet been written – perhaps Nehemiah himself had a hand in writing it down.

Whether he read on or not, his thoughts could not have been cheerful. He could not bring back those first days after the Exodus; nor was he working with the pliable economy described in Deuteronomy. Instead, he lived in barren times, with a not very united people. The depressed state of the economy probably meant that the seventh year freedom rule just did not work – it was not long enough to lay aside sufficient for independence, or perhaps the period was too short to give adequate return on a loan, and so all the credit had dried up. Anyway, it was no good looking to a seven year hope for improvement in the lot of his poor.

It is in Leviticus 25, whether read or written by Nehemiah, that we find out exactly what he did, and he fills in the background in his own book (Neh 5:1-13). If it could not be seven years, it would be seven times seven years: every fiftieth year all debts would be cancelled, and every strip of land and every house that had been sold or mortgaged in poverty would be returned to its owners. Families would get back the husbands and sons who had had to sell their freedom for food.

This would begin on the Day of Atonement in the fiftieth year, and since that day begins with a great blowing of a trumpet, it was the trumpet call that Nehemiah made the sign of restored freedom. The Hebrew word used in Leviticus for "trumpet" is *yobel*; when the translators of the Douai Bible and the Authorised Version came to that word they were not at all sure what it meant, so they spelt it in English letters: "jubilee". And jubilee it has stayed.

God's Jubilee

The Bible does not set all its ideals in tomorrow. It is a fiercely practical book for the "todays" of life. God's Jubilee must not be understood as a dream, much less as a "counsel of perfection" that can be safely ignored by the more commercial among us. Whoever invented the Jubilee knew that not much could be offered to the people; but knew even more certainly that there was a divine obligation to offer as much as was possible. It does not take proficiency in arithmetic to work out that someone who mortgages house, land, and perhaps themselves, and lives in a world where life-expectancy is short, will have little chance of seeing the fiftieth year restoration.

The Jubilee writer knew that. But the writer also knew that some would see it, and of those who did not, their children would. The writer could stop entire families and generations going into destitution; and could build into the economic system a guarantee of restoration, of dignity and of hope. And that was God's command.

Blowing our own trumpet

God's law makes people free: not only in eternity, but today. Yonder, in the New Earth, the freedom will be perfect. Here it will be limited and fragile. But God's law is not made null for us just because we cannot build paradise.

As we look at our world with its vast destitution and its deeply-rooted forms of slavery, what do we think Nehemiah would be saying to us?

He would probably become very impatient as we explained to him about market forces, or multinational imperialism, or the class struggle, or whatever we think is running the world. He would be impatient because to him it would not matter an iota (or even a yod) whether the class struggle or the "market" was the true force behind things. He would perhaps say: "If it is the class struggle, be sure that God himself owns the class struggle. You must build into it the ways in which people can experience God's own liberating rule. If, on the other hand, it is market forces, be sure that God owns them and has made you stewards of them to control them, not to let them run riot. You must build into them the times and signs of God's liberations."

The economy – however we may prefer to explain it – is given into our hands to control. We must direct it towards justice and freedom. And if we cannot establish perfect justice, that does not allow us to abandon the effort to establish as much justice as can be had in our own day. It is our job to give everyone as much hope, as much independence, and as much prosperity as we possibly can. And if the rules of the economy stand in our way, then the rules of the economy must be changed. For God's law has to be made practical and lived and trumpeted in every generation. That's what Nehemiah did; that's our job; and that's a Jubilee.

We Walk Beside the Camel

Jim O'Keefe

The Chalbi desert in northern Kenya is the home of 32,000 people belonging to the Gabbra tribe. Their "land" reaches from the Megado escarpment, just inside Ethiopia's southern boundary, southwards to Marsabit mountain, a huge volcanic outcrop capped by a magnificent forest, and the main tourist attraction in this part of Kenya. The Gabbra, who recognise no national boundaries and wander across the border into Ethiopia in search of grazing land for their animals and metal for their jewellery, lead simple lives, following their animals to the water hole and back to the grazing grounds. The two can be up to five days' walk apart, and the distance between them is increasing as the grass nearest the oasis gets used up.

The Gabbra start work before the age of seven, and stop when they get too old. The young boys and girls look after the goats and cattle. The camels, which are sacred and not to be entrusted to girls or women, are consigned to the older boys. These amazing animals can travel without food or drink for 35 days, after which, smelling water from about 7 kms, they will run towards it leaving the accompanying warrior miles behind. The curious tourist is not encouraged to photograph the camel – this could rob it of its spirit.

A long past

The history of the Gabbra is vague. Their language is not a means of written communication, so the collective memory is important. Along with the Somalis, the Rendille and the Murille, they belong to the Cushite group of tribes, which differ greatly from those of the Nilotic group (Samburu, Maasai, Luo, Turkana, etc.) and from the Bantu tribes (Kikuyu, Swahili, Ameru, etc.). But it may be that their roots are to be found in the Middle East. Some anthropologists are now suggesting that the origins of certain Old Testament customs can be traced to peoples now living in sub-Saharan Africa who once migrated south from Arabia and the surrounding regions.

Their appearance suggests that the Gabbra are a stoic people physically adapted to the life they live. With a life expectancy of about forty years, they will survive so long as they are not threatened by Western civilisation, or by anaemia and malaria, both of which are on the increase. But their existence is always precarious, not only because of their grim environment, but also because of the unbroken sequence of disasters – mainly war and disease – which has befallen them and their animals over the last century. Most recently, of course, they suffered from the severe famine that ravaged much of Africa in 1984 and 1985 and they are continually under threat from neighbouring tribesmen who come after cattle and anything else they can get.

Simple survival

The people live on a simple, high-protein diet of blood and milk which suits their extremely arduous way of life. As long as there is water nearby, an adult female camel will produce ten quarts of milk a day and their owners get blood by nicking a vein in the camel's stomach and drawing off a couple of pints – provided it has water, the camel will make up the quantity of blood quite quickly. The average family owns about twenty camels and 120 sheep and goats (one of which they may kill each month for food). Serious problems arise when the animals, on which their lives depend, die, as they do in times of famine. The people are then under threat, since the maize and corn provided by relief agencies are of little use after a diet of blood and milk.

The Gabbra are still the most nomadic of the Kenyan people. However an increasing number are settling down, and the problem for settled nomads is simple: what can they do? Their whole tradition has to do with following animals – they literally walk beside the camel – and with cooperative animal management. Those who settle down have the immediate comfort of their new way of life, but they also have to cope with long-term problems associated with unemployment. Although more than 90 per cent of the Gabbra have received no formal education, and adult literacy is less than 5 per cent, there is great resistance to education, principally, but not only, because the model of education being explored is sedentary.

Traditions and beliefs

The Gabbra tribe is made up of five clans, each with its own leadership and legal authority. The leadership, which is still in the hands of a group of circumcised men who have won the respect of the people, changes every seven years. This fascinating tradition is central to the socio-cultural identity of the people. Their understanding of the universe, measurement of time, and initiation into the next generation stage, are all understood with reference to the number seven.

The Gabbra are a very religious people, most of them animists like their forebears. One clan has been strongly influenced by Islam, but others have not. So geared are they to camel husbandry, that animal sacrifice is part of their traditional lifestyle. The head of the family is the immediate social and ritual leader and the older men act as priests whenever the people come together in groups of families or as a clan. Several times a year they will offer sacrifice and fulfil the rites of libation to ensure health, fertility and sound animals, and special sacrifices and offerings (usually of animals) are made on other occasions. They have a firm belief in an after-life, and they celebrate a rite of passage into the next life at burial. However, if one of the tribe dies as a result of war, the body is not buried. It is covered with branches to prevent wild animals from eating it. Those who die from sickness or old age are buried during a special funeral ceremony. Their relatives will sacrifice an animal which reflects the dead person's status and dignity within society, and they offer a prayer that the dead person will continue the journey safely into the next life. On the occasion of the new moon – which is always significant for the Gabbra as marking the birthday of God – the elders will pour milk into the ground as a food for those who have died, to sustain them on their journey.

The new moon is also the time for weddings and special sacrifices. A traditional Gabbra wedding can take four days. When the couple, or one of the couple, is Catholic, much of the traditional ritual is unfortunately dropped, but even in their case the feast and the dancing after the church service are very much in the traditional form.

The Gabbra have elaborate rituals for making peace. In 1985, a few months after 42 Gabbra were killed in one raid from the Rendille tribe, the elders of each tribe came together and began a process of reconciliation. They chose a piece of land near the spot where the raid had taken place and scraped a hole in the sand. They then passed their hands over the hole and placed a big stone in it. This simple ceremony meant that the quarrel was over and that the tribes were committed to live in peace. One of the elders subsequently suggested that a cross should be placed on the stone to show that their decision to make peace had been influenced by Jesus Christ.

It is not always so simple. On another recent occasion two tribes further south were trying to celebrate the making of peace by sacrificing a goat. Halfway through the ceremony one side accused the other of having stolen the goat before sacrificing it. The "peace" ceremony ended in chaos.

Thanks to the intimate relationship between their traditional lifestyle, their animal husbandry, their religious ritual and the social customs they have developed, the Gabbra have been able to maintain a balanced approach to the difficulties they face. They also have a strict moral code. If a young unmarried woman becomes pregnant, she has to leave the area with the child, and no member of her family or tribe may assist them in any way – which means that they will die unless they are taken in by another tribe. The man is not driven from the tribe, but he is effectively treated as a non-person for the rest of his life. Stealing too is anathema, as is physical violence to anyone in the tribe.

Of the Christian Churches, the Catholic has been the most effective, but in general the impact of Christianity has been minimal. Records show that while about 9 per cent of the Gabbra have been baptised into Christian denominations, only 1.5 per cent (500 people) practise. Of these, most are women and children. Catholicism has made little impact either on those influenced by Islam, or on men, who spend most of their time caring for the herds and who are unused to meeting with women and children. Originally, baptism was a sure way of receiving practical relief, an alliance that has now been discouraged! One church was known as the "church of the goat" because of the custom of giving any "new member" a goat on reception into the church – the lapsation and re-entry rate was something to behold.

The challenge to the Church

The difficulties facing a church that wants to evangelise are considerable. The nomadic life being what it is the Gabbra do not want to abandon it – and by and large the people have virtually no opportunity to meet regularly. They move about so much that the idea of meeting for "six weeks at 7.30pm in the hall" is not part of their mind-set! Distances, moreover, are great, and raids by other tribes a constant threat. Then there is the problem of dependence. The Gabbra are very poor, and to non-nomadic people their life is extremely hard. Anyone who wants to influence them in any way, anyone who seems to be making life easier for them or promises anything at all, has to be careful not to encourage dependency.

The Church must take care not to set up a conflict between its teachings and the social traditions of the Gabbra. The example of illegitimacy illustrates the problem. The role of Mary in Catholicism is a complete mystery to the Gabbra, who, with one exception, as we shall see, do not recognise the contribution of women in any public forum. Men spend their lives on the move, and in any case would not sit down and discuss anything with women in public, which suggests that very few men will be influenced by Catholicism – unless someone chooses to live alongside them as they move around the desert.

In their present form, Christian rituals, symbols and patterns of worship do not touch the lives of the

Gabbra – "joining hands" and "genuflecting" mean nothing to people who never knew the Roman Empire.

There are very few trained Gabbra catechists. Those that do exist are based in the mission stations and tend to teach in classrooms, with desks and blackboards – the presumption being that to be educated you have to live in a village and attend classes with other people. Schools have been set up near the mission station, forcing those who are interested in education to "sit still".

So the challenge to Christianity comes from Gabbra language, culture and traditional religion and, in addition, from Islam. A willingness to travel and move with the people is essential, a readiness to live with them over a period of time, immersed in their struggles and experiencing their constraints. It is easy to talk about identifying with the community but, in situations like this, extremely difficult to do so in practice. New tools of evangelisation are needed and a recognition of the way God is already working among the people. The traditional values of the warriors are under threat, the temptation to settle down is increasing, the value of education is rarely recognised. Someone needs to be very close to the fears and anxieties of the people to gain their respect and receive credibility from them.

Perhaps there has to be an ecumenical approach in the widest sense of the word – cooperation between all who are concerned about the Gabbra people and willing to work for their preservation and enhancement. It will be a long-term commitment, and any Europeans or non-local people involved will need consistent and careful support.

The Gabbra and the Jubilee

One thing that makes some anthropologists think the Gabbra may have a link with the people in the Middle East in Old Testament times is their custom of Jubilee. Every seven years the five clans send representatives into the hills in Ethiopia for four weeks. During that time, in a secret place, amid sacrifices and feasting, the new leaders are chosen and a "high" priest is elected. The people celebrate the ending of conflict, seal handshake deals with legal contracts, and reallocate animals for those in need. They put into practice the Old Testament ideal of Jubilee.

It is fascinating to talk to the Gabbra about the Jubilee. It amuses them that anyone should even ask about it. To them it is so natural. How else should problems be solved? How else should goats and camels be shared when a family loses its own in raids or through famine? How else should those in debt be freed from the burden if they have no means to pay back?

In the Old Testament the central provision of the Jubilee code was the periodic return of the people to the lands of their tribes and families. This was fundamental if Israel was to preserve its original character as an agrarian democracy. Obviously, this is not a problem for nomadic people, but the basic idea is exactly the same: everything is provided by God, all share it and no one can dominate what is available.

The Jubilee Year was an expression of the way God loves and works. God is pure gratuitousness, pure gift. As followers of Yahweh, the people had to reflect something of this gratuitousness in their lives – by cancelling debts, releasing slaves and restoring land. In other words their social, political and religious customs were to be reflections of the love of God.

Exactly the same could be said of the Gabbra. Their movement from one life stage to the next, protection of life, willingness to share animals and willingness to free from debts, are all an expression of their reverence for equality and opportunity. During their celebration of the Jubilee in the sanctuary in the hills in Ethiopia, everyone has an equal right to speak. In their normal day to day lives, women would never be asked for an opinion. In the month's celebrations, women have as much right to speak as men, their voice is heard and their judgments readily acknowledged. It is as though in the celebration there is a statement of the way things are meant to be.

Where does this leave us?

We celebrate jubilees – silver, gold, and diamond jubilees in marriage and priesthood – in recognition of "time put in" at something, as well as of the good times during those years. We call people together to celebrate the support we have received from others during the years and to give them a chance to celebrate it all with us. We recognise the gift of God in the service of others.

We are reminded of the scriptural background of the Jubilee year by Pope John Paul II in his Apostolic Letter on the millennium, *Tertio Millennio Adveniente* (TMA):

> *The jubilee year was meant to restore equality among the children of Israel, offering new possibilities to familieswhich had lost their property and even their personal freedom. On the other hand, the jubilee year was a reminder to the rich that a time would come again when their Israelite slaves would once again become their equals and would be able to reclaim their rights.... Justice, according to the Law of Israel, consisted above all in the protection of the weak. (para 13)*

The Gabbra use the celebration of the Jubilee to do precisely that – they seek to protect the weak and try to "get relationships right". In this they try to live out the ideals that are contained in the Hebrew word *shalom*. But if, for example, they are not at peace with the neighbouring tribe, they will wait another seven years to allow time to put things right, and only then will they celebrate it. Or if a particular group of young people is obviously not yet ready to assume new responsibilities, they will delay the movement into the next "life stage" – from herdsman to warrior, for example – for another seven years. Jubilee is a celebration of community, and the recognition that within the community things are going well.

Celebration is important to the people. Life is so hard, that if one family kills a goat, which it may do once a month, any other family living in the same area will be invited to join in the meal. To share is to survive. To become possessive is to threaten the social customs of the tribe and, by the same token, the tribe itself. Safety and future exist in the community and in the commitment to sharing.

The Gabbra jubilee is a statement about the gratuitousness of a God who loves, and who gives peace, prosperity, animals and children. It notes the need to illustrate this kind of activity in the lives of all the people. It is like forgiving seventy times seven, or getting up in the middle of the night to share bread because there is a need for it.

In his book *Christianity Rediscovered*, Vincent Donovan writes:

> *It is surely here, in the midst of the cultures of the world, and not in the Church, that the ordinary way to salvation must lie, the ordinary means of salvation, the very possibility of salvation for most of the human race. Or else it is a very strange God we have.*
> *(p. 30)*

Donovan is questioning the ideas of evangelisation harboured by many people over the centuries prior to Vatican II. The Gabbra, and many other tribes like them (Donovan was writing about their distant neighbours, the Maasai), challenge us to think carefully about what it is we are doing when we "evangelise". They challenge us to be acutely sensitive to their customs and traditions – these are their way to God, and we have no right to disrupt them. Donovan would say that everything about a nation has to do with salvation. He believes that it is their affair to respond to their own call of salvation. The evangelist must respect the culture of a people, not destroy it. The incarnation of the Gospel, the way in which it is given flesh and blood, is up to the people themselves.

We must begin to think of evangelisation in the areas like this, with a mind as free as possible from preconceptions and presumptions. It may be that witness is the primary stage for evangelisation, rather, even, than the wish to see people become Christians. As Pope Paul VI said in the Apostolic Exhortation *Evangelii Nuntiandi* :

> *Take a Christian or a handful of Christians who ... show their capacity for understanding and acceptance, their sharing of life and destiny with other people, their solidarity with the efforts of all for whatever is noble and good . . Through this wordless witness these Christians stir up irresistible questions in the hearts of those who see how they live.*
> *(para 21)*

Basic to any dialogue must be concern to share the Spirit of God present in each one. Paul was convinced of this presence when he wrote to the Ephesians:

> *The mystery, as it is now revealed in the Spirit to his holy apostles and prophets, was unknown to humanity in previous generations: it means that the gentiles now have the same inheritance and form the same body, and enjoy the same promise in Christ Jesus through the Gospel. (Eph 3:5-6)*

Also convinced were the bishops of Vatican II, who wrote in their Pastoral Constitution on the Church in the Modern World, *Gaudium et Spes*:

> *All this holds true not for Christians only but also for all people of good will in whose hearts grace is active invisibly. For since Christ died for all, and since all are in fact called to one and the same destiny, which is divine, we must hold that the Holy Spirit offers to all the possibility of being made partners, in a way known only to God, in the paschal mystery. (para 22)*

It has important implications for us as brothers and sisters of the Gabbra. Not only must we defend their way of life – we must also allow ourselves to be challenged by it. As representatives of the poorest people in the world, the Gabbra have things to teach us, about respect for the ecological balance of land and animals and about fairness and justice, that could profoundly affect our style of life, the way we organise our society, and the way we establish our priorities. They challenge us to alter our angle of vision so that we begin to examine our decisions with the perspective of the poorest people in our world. As long as we are unwilling to let their lifestyle and their simplicity speak to us we are colluding with an unjust and uncaring attitude which oppresses others. Either we share in their celebration of Jubilee, or we deny them the fullness of life Jesus came to bring us all (Jn 10:10).

Bridging the gap at home

But if this is true of our relations with the Gabbra in Northern Kenya, it is equally so of our relations with our fellow citizens in the British Isles. If only 8 per cent of the people in this country attend a place of worship, be it church, chapel, synagogue or mosque, at the weekend, then 92 per cent don't, and we need to explore new models of evangelisation to cope with this reality. The suggested ways in which the churches might help and support the Gabbra could equally apply to people in this country.

This is well put in the postscript to *Involvement in Community – A Christian Contribution*, published by the William Temple Foundation:

> *The gap of feeling, thinking, understanding and responding in us between the ordinary daily lives as shared with all our contemporaries and our believing has therefore to be crossed. It is*

*our calling as disciples and our task as believers –
and as theologians – to allow this gap to be
bridged. For this we need to be plunged into
the contemporary, as the ungodly experience it,
so that we may be obliged to seek and search
out how to be godly in it and how to be godly
about it.*

And again:

*A real concern for the poor must lead almost
inevitably to a restructuring of society. This
would almost certainly include the redistribution
of incomes and wealth, and the abolition of
privilege especially in education and health.
These more radical structural changes are
necessary because however much the poor are
organised they will always be weaker than the
rich. Unless privilege is reduced no deep-seated
change will occur in society which benefits
the poor.*

Some of these ideas are deepened in TMA. Pope
John Paul's emphasis is on what he calls the
"Church's preferential option for the poor and the
outcast". He goes on to say:

*A commitment to justice and peace in a world
like ours, marked by so many conflicts and
intolerable human inequalities, is a necessary
condition for the preparation and celebration of
the Jubilee ....*
(para 51)

A final thought from Pope John Paul pushes us even further in thinking how we apply the ideals of Jubilee in our time and place:

> *The eradication of poverty will only be seriously achieved when the poor themselves can take their fate into their own hands, when they become part of conceiving and putting into practice programmes that directly concern them. (Speech to Cor Unum, 27 October 1995)*

This may all sound so challenging as to be utopian. But it is no more challenging than the Year of Jubilee proclaimed in Leviticus and Deuteronomy, and lived out by Jesus after his proclamation in Luke 4: "The spirit of the Lord has been given to me, for he has anointed me ... to proclaim the Lord's year of favour."

Jubilee: An Appeal to Conversion

Jon Sobrino SJ

For every human being and certainly for the Christian, the present state of the world demands conversion. In the Jubilee context conversion involved "restoring" land, "remitting" debts and "freeing" slaves – which, in today's terms, means introducing agrarian and land reform, cancelling foreign debts or facilitating their repayment, and promoting radical and much-needed social changes.

Our task here is not to analyse what this means in practical detail but rather to set out the basic forms conversion will have to take if Jubilee is to be possible. So, taking faith as our starting point, the first thing we must do is to return to the truth about this world.

There is no point in proclaiming a Jubilee unless we are aware of the evils it is supposed to remedy. Today, it is not just that isolated aspects of the world are evil or that individual countries are going through hard times. God's creation as a whole is affected. Our world embodies neither the ideal God had when he created it for all (cf Gen 1:18-20), nor his vision for its future, in which all would work and enjoy the fruits of their labour (cf Is 65:21-22).

Indeed, not only does the world not embody this ideal and this vision, it denies them to the majority of the human race. Thus, what is evil is the widespread existence of poverty and the fact that poor people are always condemned to the slow death induced by the present world order. This then, is the first assertion that can be made about the reality of our world: that the majority of men and women live in poverty, closer to death than to life.

This state of affairs must be unambiguously denounced. Poverty is not inevitable in today's world; it is the product of history, or, in religious terms, it is structural sin. Poverty has a cause. By and large, it is the result of the injustice which dominates the economies of many individual countries, and the economy of the world as a whole. It is, as the Latin American bishops have said, institutionalised violence, the most serious and the most clearly self-perpetuating of all forms of violence. From this point of view, the poor resemble the suffering servant of Yahweh, burdened with the sin, the injustice, the selfishness and the indifference of the world.

Finally, this world must be exposed for what it is, because like all sin it tries to pass for something it is not. We need to expose the way in which human creations such as democracy, security, Western Christendom – legitimate and potentially positive in themselves – are used to obscure the truth about how things are. We need to unmask the fiction that the human race as a whole is moving forward towards reason, freedom and life – this is true, and then no more than partially so, only of a minority of the human race.

To become converted to the truth, to see things as they are in themselves and recognise their causes, to act on what we have seen, is the most important thing the world demands of us. Terrified though we may be at the sight of the world we have built with our hands, if we do not start here, we will not be able to hear the good news of Jubilee. Instead we will hear the voice of God's anger: "The wrath of God will be revealed against those who imprison the truth with injustice" (Rom 1:18). No matter how tragic, we must start from the truth about our world: define it as *poverty* which leads to death, denounce it as *sin* and unmask as a *lie* the mechanisms that try to hide its truth.

Effective compassion towards the poor

This being so, Jubilee demands first a conversion in reaction against the world of sin, which in the language of the Beatitudes can be described as mercy or compassion. To be compassionate is to be deeply moved by tragedy and to respond to it through service. Compassion is not only or primarily a feeling; rather, it is a response from something deep within our being. It derives its strength from the fact that, having internalised that same reality, we are moved to respond.

When, in the gospels, Jesus comes up against the suffering of others his first reaction is heartfelt compassion. And when he wants to indicate a complete human being, he points to the Samaritan and describes him as one who is moved to compassion (Lk 10:33).

Our compassion is effective when we work to transform the world of sin with signs of the Kingdom of God, by meeting the real needs of those who suffer. This is what we do whenever we try to relieve suffering caused by earthquakes, drought, human rights violations, wars, and so on.

This practical compassion in the face of suffering must be accompanied by work to build structures better suited to the Kingdom of God. In other words, love for individuals must go hand in hand with a structural, political love which seeks to transform the international order so that the countries of the Third World can have life. It is not easy to sustain compassion like this. Anyone with a compassionate heart will meet with persecution. Compassion like that of Jesus, or of Martin Luther King, or of Archbishop Romero, is a threat to those who respond to tragedy with hearts of stone. It must therefore be strong enough to carry conviction and persevere to the end – which is what gives it credibility in the eyes of those towards whom 'it is directed. For if compassion denotes tenderness and heartfelt concern at the suffering of others, it also denotes strength, powerful denunciation of oppressors, and courage to stand firm when the latter come back to oppress those who defend the poor.

Compassion must be accompanied, moreover, by a particular attitude of mind. In the first place, it must be exercised with gratitude. Opportunities for showing compassion inevitably arise out of tragedy; but once they do arise, those who help the poor must be thankful that they have been given the chance to do so. Secondly, compassion must be exercised as reparation. Structurally speaking there can be no doubt that the sufferings of the poor are inflicted on them by the world of wealth and power. Turning to them in order to help is not merely to give them something; it is to give them back what is theirs. Jubilee is more than a proclamation of compassion; it is a recognition of the obligation to make amends.

Solidarity: Good News for all

When the world shows compassion as I have described it, strong, effective, and accompanied by the joy of gratitude and by the humility of reparation, then it is proclaiming Jubilee. It is announcing good news to the poor – and not only to them but also to the world which has given them life. The Jubilee which begins by demanding conversion also offers salvation.

It is not uncommon for those who help the poor to feel that they are the ones who are being helped, that in giving they receive. Although the exchange appears to favour the poor, in reality it moves in both directions. The poor to whom salvation is offered offer salvation to the rest of us.

In the first place, the poor give a new and positive sense of life to a world dehumanised by oppression and indifference, and by an illusion of progress. In the crucified people of today there is light (Is 42:6; 49:6) and salvation (Is 53:11), as there was in the servant of Yahweh described by Isaiah, and in the crucified Christ. This may seem an outrageous statement, but is invariably found to be true by those who really get to know the poor. These people are closer to the reality of things; but if their sufferings are more real, so is their hope. The great service they offer us is simply to situate us within the world as it is and hence within the truth; and in so doing they give us back the dignity we have lost in a world of sin and untruth. It may seem a small thing, but by making us citizens of a real rather than of a fictitious and sinful world, the poor put meaning and happiness back into life, they restore to us the essence of our humanity.

Secondly, the poor receive us. Surprisingly enough, they admit us to their table, who for centuries have, structurally speaking, been their oppressors. Instead of complaining that we have turned up late they open their arms in welcome. They offer us fraternity and communion; they help us overcome not only our exclusiveness and our insularity but also the seemingly unbridgeable gulf between oppressors and oppressed. Their welcome brings reconciliation and consequently salvation.

In short, the poor forgive us, which is something we need to bear in mind when we speak of Jubilee. At a time of Jubilee the debts of the poor are cancelled, which is good news for them. But what we have to ask in all honesty is what debt is it that really needs to be cancelled, who is in greater need of forgiveness, who forgives whom? John Paul II has said that on judgement day the countries of the Third World will judge those of the First World. But the Third World is already burdened with the sin of the First World, and in that sense it is not its debtor but its creditor. It is up to the Third World to forgive, not the other way round, and it is ready to do so. The Third World is a place of sin, but also a place of forgiveness.

The forgiveness granted by the poor is a great gift. A world which does not recognise its sinfulness is not living in the truth. Through their forgiveness the poor bring to light the sin of the First World – as Karl Rahner has said, only those who are forgiven know that they are sinners. But because they expose our sinfulness in an act of forgiveness, we are not paralysed by the revelation. Many of those who have come closer to the poor have found liberation in this simultaneous experience of themselves as sinful and as forgiven. They have recovered their hope and committed themselves wholeheartedly to the service of others. As in the parable of the prodigal son, the encounter has, against all expectations, been a joyful one. The poor have been the mediators of God's forgiveness.

Thirdly, the poor help us to reformulate our ideas and compel us to work towards a utopia, so that the world can be made human for all who live in it. By the way in which they are forced to live they demonstrate to us that the world will never become more human if it insists on directing its energies towards the kind of "progress" which fosters division between peoples, impoverishes the Third World, and perverts the spirit of brotherhood: in short, a world which gives birth to the anti-kingdom instead of the Kingdom of God. The poor offer us the ideal of a simple, austere, even poor world, where the goods of the earth are shared and the values of solidarity and community are paramount.

Such a utopia offers us "the human way of life" in place of the "western way of life", which many are now beginning to question. As a utopia *(ou-topos)*, it would seem that there is no place for it in the world. But the poor point the way to it and give us strength for the journey, so that it can find a place in history. In any case, this utopia of the poor is what humanises history, makes it give more of itself, and creates for the future incomplete yet humanising utopias – small expressions of solidarity, seeds of freedom, signs of generosity and commitment. And we have to ask ourselves what the world should expect if none of this is realised.

Finally, the poor provide believers with the context and content for their faith in God, and hence with the opportunity to turn their lives into lives of faith. Since the poor are the direct recipients of the revelation of God, it is from them that we come to know what is unique and original in God and also what is unsettling about God. From the standpoint of the poor, faith can become impossible, because it seems so irrational, but it can also become, for the first time perhaps, real faith in the real God, as God is revealed to us.

From the poor we learn that God's revelation is essentially partisan and only indirectly universal. God is revealed as their saviour and liberator, as having made an option for them. The revelation takes place within and not prior to this option for the poor. We do not know God first and then learn of this option: in the act of revelation God makes this choice for the poor, and in that choice God is revealed. This theme runs through Scripture, from the moment of God's initial revelation in Exodus, as liberator of the oppressed, whose cries God has heard (Ex 3:7-10) to the eschatological revelation in Jesus, in whom God comes close in a Kingdom which is designed specifically for the poor (Lk 6:20). This bias is implicit in the creeds of Israel and appears in what can be described as historical definitions of God: "Father of orphans and widows is God" (Ps 68:5); "in you the orphan finds compassion" (Hos 14:3); a liberator (Ex 3:7-10).

This partisan God is presents as an exclusive choice and as essentially opposed to other divinities, which, instead of defending the oppressed, hasten their death. Thus true faith in God is always faith in the God of life. It is and must be genuinely anti-idolatrous, working against those dead idols which need victims – the poor – for their survival. That is why we are forbidden to worship idols, to treat Yahweh's "rivals" as gods. This partisan God, opposed by nature to idolatry, identifies with the victims of idols and dwells within them. God is to be found in history in the cries of the poor, in the sufferings of the servant and the cross of Jesus, in all who are weak, needy and insignificant (Mt 25:31-46).

That God is like this is not something we discover through our natural reason, which means that faith in God exists in a state of constant tension. In a world where faith is no longer a part of the general culture, belief in such a God tends to seem absurd, with the result that faith tends to be rejected; or outrageous, leaving protest as the only possible response; or else illusory, in which case faith may be abandoned. There are always other, more universal gods in which to believe, gods more consistent with the mystery as human beings perceive it; or we can abandon faith altogether, and simply resign ourselves to the human condition.

For the poor, however, there can be no faith apart from faith in this God. And they have that faith: they believe in a liberating God, who has known limitations and suffering; in a God who dies among human beings and yet is the God of life. This is the faith they offer to us all. We may or may not accept it, but the fact remains that only through the poor does it acquire its intrinsic meaning.

This is why many of those who have lived among and come to know the poor claim to have recovered or reaffirmed their Christian faith. God remains a mystery. In the language of tradition God is revealed as the "Almighty Other". But God is known as Other only after being encountered first as the "God of the poor". Without being able to explain why, these people justify their faith in this ultimate mystery on the grounds that for the poor hope continues to prove a wiser response than resignation or desperation, love stronger than egoism, and that giving one's life for the life of the poor is more fulfilling than keeping it for oneself.

In the midst of the poor it becomes clearer that life must be lived in hope, in love and in commitment. This is what faith in God is about; by living like this, we become better attuned to the reality of God, and life can be understood from within, as a journeying with God through history.

What the poor offer is therefore of a different order from what they receive when Jubilee is proclaimed for them: they offer life that has meaning and they offer faith. The solidarity between those who give and those who receive touches the furthermost limits of human existence. Jubilee is urgently needed if the poor of this world are to have life; but it must be put into practice for the sake of the world as a whole so that life can be given back its meaning.

Jubilee for El Salvador

El Salvador is a nation that has been torn apart and crucified by war, but it is also a symbol of the Third World which hopes for and demands a Jubilee and which cries out for solidarity. Its needs reach far beyond short-term emergency relief. Its crisis is long-lasting and structural. That is why a lasting Jubilee is required, proclaiming the possibility of life – and that is much more difficult than a special "Jubilee event".

It would be unrealistic to imagine that the First World is going to commit itself permanently to the Jubilee ideal, but this is something we must strive for. To gain encouragement, we must always bear in mind the words of Archbishop Romero: "Let it not be forgotten that we are human beings."

This is what Jubilee is about, the obligation not to forget those who have been crucified, because to forget them is to forget our humanity, to become dehumanised.

But El Salvador is also an example and a symbol of the living hope of crucified peoples. Amidst the rubble there is life, generosity and hope. Once again the people want to return to life. And in the aftermath of war, faced with enormous obstacles as they strive to bring reconciliation, the people keep on praying, working, organising to renew a dialogue which will lead to peace and justice.

This living hope is what crucified peoples offer us and that is why Jubilee is also good news for all. The poor make us share in their faith and their hope.

Reclaiming the Scapegoat

Brian Davies

> After weeks of getting ready and several delays,
> the green light was finally given for 25
> November. At around 3am the buses arrived to
> take us to Nong Khai at the Thai border. In all
> we were 127 (including 4 disabled), together
> with a number of bicycles and chickens. We had
> to wait nearly an hour because the customs
> office on the Lao side is closed at midday. So at
> about 1.30pm the buses went down onto the
> ferry and our friends went on foot. I think that
> is the most beautiful image I have of this return:
> the refugees, among whom are a number of
> children and young people, standing up and
> staring wide-eyed at the Mekong River –
> certainly the first time many had seen it....
>
> That evening, "my families" headed off for their
> new village. I am happy and thank God that
> finally they are starting their real life in their
> own place.
>
> (Sr Pierre Marie Bail, Sister of Charity, working
> with Jesuit Refugee Service in Thailand)

The homecoming of refugees is a very special
experience – returning to their own country and

their own people, discovering anew how it feels to be free, at ease and "in their own place". Many younger returnees have only ever been, all their lives, in refugee camps, constantly wary that what little they have could so easily be taken away from them and that they might, at any moment, have to uproot, move on, and begin the process of establishing a community all over again in a new camp.

For some the homecoming would be less organised and more hazardous – never quite sure about mine-fields along the route, or whether their government was truly respecting human rights again. The actual home might have been destroyed in war and need to be rebuilt. It might only be on reaching their native town or village that people discover who has actually survived. The welcome home might be marred by sadness about those who perished or who have returned terribly disabled. But it is only with the passage of time that the returnees will be able to discern whether the deeper causes of alienation in their society that were responsible for their being refugees in the first place have been dealt with.

Like the human rights worker freed from prison, the child liberated from the garment factory or from prostitution and the peasant-farmer restored to the land, the refugee who no longer needs asylum and returns home is a proclamation of the Lord's favour, a sign of Jubilee and a cause for celebration. In each of these cases, however, we may ask how far there has been genuine reconciliation. It is not enough simply to be physically free: before reconciliation can take place there has to be some recognition of the nature of the oppression that took place and those responsible need to acknowledge the part they have played. This recognition of failure, in religious terms called 'sin', together with repentance and change of heart makes possible the reconciliation to which we are called. It also makes more likely the change in the structures needed to prevent the oppression or anything like it continuing. We can understand, therefore, the importance to the new South Africa of having, not just a War Crimes Tribunal, but a Truth Commission whose purpose is far more profound than simply to convict the oppressors of their crime.

What is involved in reconciliation is not just a matter of "forgive and forget". Of course, we should forgive – however difficult that may be for those who have suffered – but we should also remember, if by that we understand the need to deal with the original causes of alienation and to see that they are not repeated.

Reconciliation and Jubilee

To understand the connection between reconciliation and Jubilee we need to examine the context for the celebration of Jubilee in the Old Testament. We have already seen in the earlier chapters by Aloys Opiyo and Jon Sobrino that celebrating the Jubilee involved restoring land, remitting debts and freeing slaves since these represented the most significant ways in which inequality and division had grown up. Those who had accumulated more were to give it back in observance of the holiness code set out in Leviticus. But how did the law come to be presented in this way? And what had such mundane matters to do with holiness and a restored relationship with God?

The biblical story traces the growing division between rich and poor to the abandonment by Israel of its original inspiration to be an alternative society of freedom and solidarity in contrast to the other kingdoms and empires of the region. It had instead adopted the kingship system. In the northern kingdom of Israel the prophets Amos and Hosea criticised the injustice not just of individual acts by people in power but of the whole system that was producing extreme luxury for the court and upper class and poverty for the country population. Similarly, in the southern kingdom of Judah, Isaiah and Micah criticised the structures responsible for causing such hardship among country people and the urban poor while those at the top lived off the fat of the land.

But it was not till after the collapse of the kingship system and the Babylonian exile that there was a concerted effort to learn from the disaster of the past. The return from exile was to be a break with the political power of the king and the ideological link with cult which had only brought economic oppression and idolatry. Now there was to be a new Exodus, a new beginning with Yahweh as king, the hallowing of cult, economic equality and political self-determination for the people. (These were the hopes of second Isaiah and Ezechiel.) The concern of the prophets was to prevent sin becoming part of the structures again: it had to be named, confessed and cast out of the community.

After fifty years in exile, all families were to receive the same gift of land to enable them to make a living – just as they had under the original egalitarian system. This is the background for the Jubilee Year of Leviticus 25 which sets out the details of how inequality that had grown up over the years was to be addressed. The context of this passage is important: it is part of the Holiness Code (chapters 17-26), the set of laws to which obedience is demanded to show that Israel belongs to Yahweh and is therefore a holy people. These laws are linked with the liturgy of the Day of Atonement to be found in Leviticus 16 within the setting of strict cultic observance.

After sacrificing a goat for the sin of the people, Aaron:

> *is to bring the other goat that is still alive ... lay his hands on its head and confess all the faults of the sons of Israel, all their transgression and all their sins, and lay them to its charge. Having thus laid them on the goat's head, he shall send it out into the desert led by a man waiting ready, and the goat will bear all their faults away with it into a desert place.*
> *(Lev 16:20-22)*

So during the great feast of Yom Kippur (Atonement) the public, structural sin of Israel is identified and confessed, a Jubilee year inaugurated and new relationships made possible. The key point for us is that we are not dealing here with any "cheap" reconciliation which pretends that all will be well if we pray for God's forgiveness but which leaves the power relationships as they were. The Day of Atonement or Reconciliation involves the naming of sin and (in the Holiness Code) specific practical action to deal with the systems responsible – all expressed in a symbolic liturgical ritual. The rite of the scapegoat, far from being an act of escapism dodging responsibility and placing the blame upon an innocent party, was a way of acknowledging the sins of the community. Their removal and the reconciliation with God were linked with commitment to a new code of behaviour.

Reconciliation and Structural Sin

Like the Day of Atonement, the Great Jubilee of the Year 2000 is also to be an occasion for acknowledging the sins of our community. In his Apostolic Letter *Tertio Millennio Adveniente* (TMA) Pope John Paul II asks us to recall all those times when the Church's children "indulged in ways of thinking and acting which were truly forms of counter-witness and scandal" (para 33). Among these Pope John Paul draws special attention to those sins "which have been detrimental to the unity willed by God for his people." These have caused the Christian community to be painfully wounded, contradicting the will of Christ and giving scandal to the world. Therefore we must ask forgiveness and make amends in order to overcome the divisions of the past, while we pray even more earnestly for Christian unity (para 34).

The second area of structural sin on which the Church is called to repentance is that of "intolerance and even the use of violence in the service of truth." Even though there may have been mitigating circumstances this "does not exonerate the Church from the obligation to express profound regret for the weaknesses of so many of her sons and daughters who sullied her face" (para 35).

Thirdly there should be an examination of conscience on the responsibility which the Church shares for the evils of our day – religious indifference, the violation of human rights, and "grave forms of injustice and exclusion." And the Pope adds : "It must be asked how many Christians really know and put into practice the principle of the Church's social doctrine." (para 36). John Paul II is clearly referring here to such widespread social evils as racism, sexism and international debt in which most of us are implicated.

These are all serious matters on which the Pope makes a frank confession of the Church's failure. He does so in order that we can identify the sin for ourselves and so eliminate it from the community. Referring to the 1984 Synod on Penance and

Reconciliation, he emphasises the need for "conversion" or *metanoia* which is the pre-condition for reconciliation with God on the part of both individuals and communities." We will then be able to share in the joy of the Jubilee, "a joy based upon the forgiveness of sins, the joy of conversion" (TMA, para 32).

The 1984 Synod to which we have just referred had difficulty in accepting the idea of structural sin because it seemed to minimise the significance of individual responsibility and hence of personal sin. John Paul II in his subsequent Apostolic Exhortation *Reconciliatio et Paenitentia* therefore clarified the matter:

> *Whenever the Church speaks of situations of sin, or when she condemns as social sins certain situations or the collective behaviour of certain groups, big or small, or even of whole nations and blocks of nations, she knows and she proclaims that such cases of social sin are the result of the accumulation and concentration of many personal sins .... The real responsibility then lies with individuals.*
> *(para 16)*

Nevertheless, the idea of structural sin is taken up and further explored in the Pope's 1987 Encyclical Letter on Social Concern, *Sollicitudo Rei Socialis*:

> *A world which is divided into blocks, sustained by rigid ideologies and in which instead of interdependence and solidarity different forms*

of imperialism hold sway, can only be a world
subject to structures of sin.
(para 36)

It is essential to be able to point to the true nature
of the evil which faces us. John Paul II goes on to
identify two sinful attitudes which are very typical:
the all-consuming desire for profit and the thirst for
power:

Not only individuals fall victim to this double
attitude of sin; nations and blocks do so too.
And this favours even more the introduction of
the "structures of sin" of which I have spoken.
(TMA, para 37)

In TMA he goes so far as to apply the idea to the
Church.

In what is being proposed, then, as part of our
preparation for the Great Jubilee, we have been
presented in TMA with a number of examples of
structural sin in which we have been caught up as a
community. The effects of these sins in social terms
have been felt by us all. Now we are to acknowledge
them, express our repentance for any shame we
have had in contributing to them, and ensure that
changes are made in the structures so that they do
not recur. All this is necessary if we are to be fully
reconciled with God and our fellow women and
men. The problem is that we have no appropriate
ritual expression for such reconciliation to take
place of the kind that was provided by the scapegoat
and the associated liturgy.

Celebrating our reconciliation with the community

Those who can still recall their old catechism answers will know that the sacrament of penance involves four elements: contrition, confession and satisfaction – on the part of the penitent, and absolution – on the part of the priest. Following the liturgical reforms of the Second Vatican Council, the new rite of 1973 began to speak of "the sacrament of reconciliation" and to find ways of making these four elements more significant. The emphasis on inner conversion and being conformed to Christ of course remains, but there was a new recognition that, since we are all joined together, the sin of one is harmful to others. "In this way, penance always implies reconciliation with one's fellow human beings who have suffered the effects of our sins" (New Order of Penance, para 5).

The element that has been most problematic is "satisfaction", ie the amendment of our life for the future and the reparation for any damage caused by sin. "That order which has been harmed must be restored and the sickness responsible for the sin must be healed by means of a suitable remedy" (New Order of Penance, para 6). It is hard enough to work out how this is to be done, making reparation and amending our lives, with regard to our more personal failings but the real difficulty is in making amends for social sin. Indeed, as we have seen, the difficulty is often in recognising that we are implicated in social sin in the first place.

So what can be done? The purpose of this chapter has been to highlight the need for an appropriate rite of reconciliation and it is only possible to outline some suggestions of how this might be met.

First, far more use could be made of services of reconciliation which could focus on social sin and the ways in which we may be responsible for at least some of the ills of our society. The New Order of Penance saw such services as an opportunity to remind the congregation of "the social aspect of grace and sin, by which every act of the individual in some way has its repercussion on the whole body of the Church." It also emphasised the importance of "doing works which show a real charity towards God and our fellow men and women" (New Order of Penance, para 26). The rite of reconciliation could involve a public act of confession for social sin, of trust in God's mercy – recognising that God's grace is also at work in the structures of this world – and of commitment to live according to a new code of social behaviour.

Secondly, we need to bear in mind that *the* sacrament of reconciliation is the Eucharist, where Christ's sacrifice which has reconciled us with God is made present. After all, Christ is not only our paschal lamb but at the same time our scapegoat who takes away the sins of the world. At the beginning of Mass there is a brief penitential rite that could occasionally be extended so as to include an examination of conscience on the sort of social issues elaborated by Pope John Paul. This would seem to be no more than applying Matthew 5:23-24 to the context of structural sin. "So then if you are bringing your offering to the altar and there remember that your brother (or sister) has something against you, leave your offering there before the altar, go and be reconciled with your brother (or sister) first, and then come back and present your offering." In effect this would be to combine the celebration of Mass with a service of reconciliation in the way proposed by J.D. Crichton in *The Ministry of Reconciliation* (1974). Such an approach to the Eucharist for a special occasion would also underline the power of the Eucharist in social issues.

Thirdly, CAFOD is proposing to the Church in England and Wales to renew their commitment to the poor of the Third World by sharing in "A New Covenant with the Poor". This could be seen as part of the preparation for the millennium in each diocese and perhaps in each parish. Whatever the details of the individual covenants drawn up by dioceses, parishes, Catholic organisations or schools, they would contribute a particular way in which reconciliation could be seen to be taking place. It would go very well with the special liturgy outlined above, giving it something of the role of a holiness code in our reconciliation for the Great Jubilee of the Year 2000.